## COLLECTORS GUIDES

# POST CARDS

Text©        Martin Willoughby
Illustration© Phillips Fine Art
             Auctioneers
Edited by     Emma Sinclair-Webb
Designed by   Strange Design Associates

Copyright © Dunestyle Publishing Ltd and
Boxtree Ltd, 1989

Boxtree Ltd.
36 Tavistock Street
London WC2 7PB

Conceived by Dunestyle Publishing Ltd

ISBN 1 85283 251 7

Typesetting by O'Reilly Clark, London
Colour separation by Chroma Graphics
(Overseas) Pte Ltd
Printed In Italy by New Interlitho spa.

# Phillips
## COLLECTORS GUIDES

# POST CARDS

CAIRO
Arabic Bazar

MARTIN WILLOUGHBY

**BOXTREE**

**Phillips**
WEST TWO

Phillips, founded in 1796, has a reputation for specialisation. Its specialists handle fine art, antiques and collectors' items under more than 60 subject headings — a huge spectrum of art and artefacts that ranges from Old Masters and the finest antique furniture to cigarette cards and comparatively modern pop memorabilia. The auction group's Collectors' Centre, situated at Phillips West Two in Salem Road, Bayswater, London, is constantly recognising, defining and catering for new trends in collecting. It answers hundreds of queries a day from collectors, museums, dealers and the public at large. The shelves of its cataloguing halls are packed with a treasure-trove of objects, awaiting their turn to appear at auction. To varying extents, the scene there and in the main Mayfair salerooms (Phillips, 7 Blenheim Street, London W1Y 0AS; telephone 01-629 6602) is repeated at a score of Phillips branches elsewhere in Britain.

Phillips West 2
10 Salem Road
London W2 4BU
Telephone: 01-221 5303

Contents

# Introduction

Postmark: 14 November 1905
Hamilton, Scotland.
Ruby,
Our lips shall meet
In kisses sweet
At 8.15 to-night.    XXX

Postmark: 22 March 1906
London.
My Dear Maud,
George came round today; of course we are all disgusted with him. Had a rotton *(sic)* day at the office. Best wishes, Gertie.

Unfortunately we will never know the identity of Ruby's mysterious suitor (was he a decent sort of chap or just a despicable cad?) and what exactly did George do that disgusted Gertie so much? Whatever the answers, it is messages such as these, scribbled on the backs of postcards, that bring to life those days when the craze for sending pictures through the post took hold of the world. Whether it was for holiday greetings or cryptic messages, for arranging a trip to the theatre or a lover's moonlit meeting, there was a time when the postcard would have been the automatic choice.

This book focuses mainly on the brief period in history from the

*Below* Edwardian elegance, as depicted on this postcard of a hotel interior, was a recurring theme with publishers and gave the impression of a wealthy and ordered society. In fact, the years between 1900 and 1914 were a time of change and unrest.

end of Queen Victoria's reign up to the beginning of the First World War — the period regarded as the heyday of the picture postcard. The majority of the cards most collected today date from this decade-and-a-half at the beginning of the twentieth century (with some obvious exceptions mentioned further on in the book). The events depicted on postcards from all nations reflect the preoccupations and news stories of the time; the subjects represented are those that were close to the people's hearts.

Before the telephone became standard equipment in every household, the picture postcard was ready-at-hand as the simplest, cheapest and most attractive method of communcation. It was fairly quick too — not uncommon are messages reading along the lines of 'See you for tea this afternoon at 4.30', on cards sent to a neighbouring town and post-marked earlier that same morning. Very often, though, cards were sent merely as additions to the recipient's album; 'Sent with affection, to swell your

collection', reads one particular example sent in 1907. In fact, so many cards were sent to swell the collections of friends and relatives that, at the peak of their usage, over two million were travelling through the post in Great Britain PER DAY! Up until 1918 the postage rate for cards was a halfpenny and almost all the cards would bear one of the green halfpenny stamps of the period. The sheer abundance of cards, and hence stamps, makes it highly unlikely that the stamps are of value in their own right as collectors' items. The end of the First World War found a nation in more serious mood and, with the doubling of the postage rate, the torrential flow of postcards was reduced to a trickle. It took another sixty years or so before collecting these small rectangular pieces of cardboard was to rank again as one of the country's leading collecting hobbies.

Most postcard catalogues and guides list somewhat in excess of fifty main categories or subjects

and hundreds more sub-categories into which cards can be grouped. To do each one justice each category really deserves a chapter to itself, if the phenomenal output of the Edwardian postcard publishers is to be covered. However, allowing for the confines of space, I have decided to introduce the new collector and those who are thinking of taking up the hobby to what is available, by briefly covering some of the more popular areas of collecting,

followed by a personal selection of 'the best of the rest'. The collector today has ample opportunity to specialize in themes as diverse as shipping, political, royalty, animals, advertising, comic and embroidered silk postcards; even obscure subjects, such as corkscrews, letters of the alphabet, typewriters, Dickens'characters and Santa Claus, appear on the picture postcard.

So, where do you start looking?

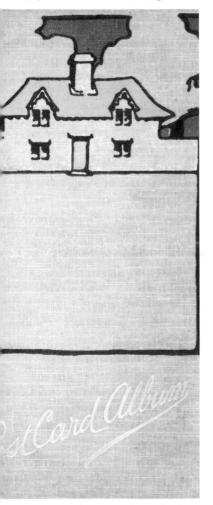

*Left* Many Edwardian households owned postcard albums, which were sometimes as decorative as the cards they contained.

*Below* Raphael Tuck & Sons were acknowledged as
the leaders in publishing creative, quality postcards.
This advertisement appeared in a theatrical magazine
early in 1904.

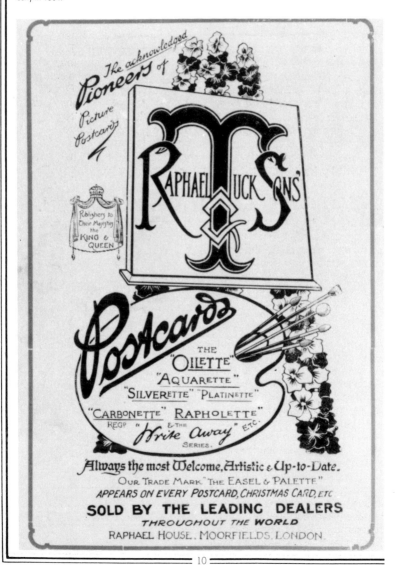

Probably the best place is at one of the regular postcard fairs held up and down the country. Here a number of dealers (up to one hundred and fifty at the major London events) gather with all their postcard stocks, to buy and sell. Most cards will be grouped into their various categories and priced in pencil on the backs. It is simply a matter of looking through the categories that appeal to you and buying those whose prices you are happy with. I feel that postcard collecting is still a relatively cheap hobby to pursue. The best cards are around £30-£100/$54–$180 plus; there are plenty in the £3-£10/$5-$18 price range and, on certain subjects, a reasonable collection could be put together for less than £3/$5 a card. In most other collecting fields the best items can easily cost thousands and certainly not much can be found for as little as a pound or two. Auctions are another good source of material. They are held at regular intervals by several auction houses around the country, with Phillips in London to the fore in this field. Top quality single cards and sets, specialized collections and general assortments can usually be found in these popular sales, ensuring something for everyone. The collector will find that, as his collection grows, his specialist knowledge will grow with it, so he may wish to write up his collection and detail the circumstances under which particular cards were issued. On the other hand many collectors are perfectly happy buying cards simply to look at the pictures! Either way, a wide variety of literature is available for those wishing to take advantage of it, and includes many specialized books by knowledgeable collectors; annually-published catalogues give price-guides to all the different types of cards available (those published by I.P.M. Publications and R. F. Postcards give a good indication of current market prices and trends); and magazine *Picture Postcard Monthly* contains news items and articles and lists forthcoming events on the postcard scene.

Firstly, however, let us go back to the origins of the postcard.

# Chapter One

# Early Days

In the mid-1860s both Heinrich von Stephen (a German) and Dr. Emmanuel Hermann (an Austrian) separately had the idea of producing a leaflet, or card, that could be sent through the post, with a message written on one side and the address on the other, no envelope being needed. The Austrian government accepted Hermann's idea and on 1st October 1869 they issued the first correspondence card to be followed exactly a year later by the first British postcard, pre-printed with a stamp and ready for sending: cost to the public — a halfpenny each.

However, these early postal-stationery cards (as they are known) did not bear the pictures and scenic views looked for by today's collectors; in fact they were rather dull by comparison, the address having to be written on one side while the other side

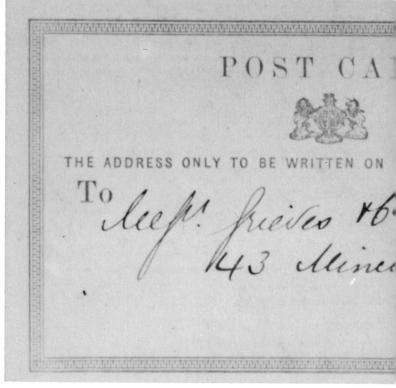

POST CA

THE ADDRESS ONLY TO BE WRITTEN ON

To *Mess.* *friedes* *&6*
*143 Mine*

was left blank for the message. The new method of communication did, however, prove extremely popular and hundreds of thousands were posted on the first day alone. Because so many were sent, these early cards are not uncommon today and can be picked up for a pound or two, although to find one of those actually postmarked on the first day of sale (1st October 1870) is more difficult as many

*Left* An example of the first British postal-stationery card, used on the first day of issue (October 1st 1870).

have been lost in the intervening century or so. Today an example would cost around £200/$360.

There was some worry for a time after the introduction of the postcard that sending an 'open' message, which could be read by all, might offend the recipient. Some traders even threatened those who had not paid their bills that, unless the money was forthcoming, a demand would be

*Below* A German *'Gruss Aus . . .'* card. Note how the view vignette leaves room for a short messeage on the picture side.

sent on a postcard for all the world to see! Traders were also quick to see the advertising potential of the new cards and examples can be found with overprints publicizing a range of company names.

The development of the postcard proceeded quite slowly, with little happening over the next twenty years. Special cards, still in the same format, were produced to commemorate the Jubilee of penny postage in 1890 and the Royal Naval Exhibition at Eddystone Lighthouse in 1891 (examples of which could be purchased and sent from the lighthouse with a special post-mark). However, it was not until 1894 that the next milestone was reached. Privately printed postcards, not bearing pre-printed stamps but requiring the sender to attach a halfpenny

stamp, were allowed from 1st September of that year. With the advent of these private cards, pictures started to appear on the message side; the birth of the picture postcard in Britain had truly taken place.

At this time the message was still restricted to one side of the card and the address to the other. Therefore, in order to leave enough room for the sender to write a few words, the pictures could not take up the whole of the available space. This gave rise to 'vignettes' — small views that would cover only a third or a half of the message area — which left the sender room enough to wish Aunt Gertie a happy birthday or tell Uncle George how nice the weather was. The size of these cards came to be known as 'court size' and measured 4½ x 3½

*Below* Vignette views on a card commemorating Victoria's sixty years as Queen. Down the left hand side it reads 'Designed in England, Printed in Germany', confirming the latter's superior printing techniques at the time.

inches (115 x 89 mm). Post Offices in Europe allowed cards a full inch longer, which increased the area by nearly 25 per cent. So, when the British Post Office finally accepted the larger cards 5½ x 3½ inches (140 x 89 mm), on 1st November 1899, it meant there was more room for better pictures and the sender had enough space to send greetings to Aunt Gertie AND Uncle George on the card.

The final step in the development of the British postcard came about in 1902. From 1st January, the 'divided back' was permitted. A vertical line was drawn centrally down the back of the card, allowing the address to be written below the stamp, on the right-hand side, with the message occupying the space to the left. Therefore, the whole of the other side was now available

*Below* A selection of fine Art Nouveau and Art Deco cards including several by Alphonse Mucha.

for the picture; publishers were quick to take advantage, although the old style 'undivided backs' could still be found in use over the next few years.

The early cards so far described can form an interesting collection, with room for further study. In Europe and particularly Germany, during the latter part of the last century, many cards were produced with view vignettes of a particular town and the words *'Gruss aus . . .'* (greetings from) with the town name. These and similar cards are still fairly inexpensive in this country, being more popular on the continent. About £3/$5 each would be an average starting price, although, for postally-used cards, the earlier the usage, the scarcer the card will be; a premium would have to be paid for pre-1895 examples.

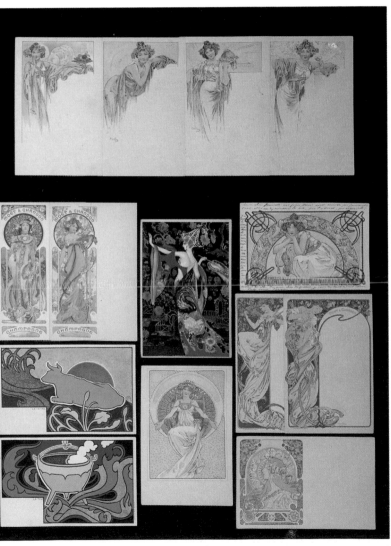

*Below* Designed by Elizabeth Suntrel in the early part of the century and valued at around £25/$45.

With the introduction of the divided back the flood-gates opened and the golden age of the postcard began. The standardization of card size enabled albums to be made in which to keep them, and it seemed that every household possessed such an album. The Edwardians went postcard crazy and would send cards to each other just as we would make phone calls today. Seaside holidays, birthdays, journeys, arrivals and departures and visits to the theatre would all be recorded by the sending of a postcard. However, the early usage of picture postcards in Germany had given them a head start in printing techniques, resulting in many of the top-quality colour printed cards of the early Edwardian years being printed in that country, using the chromo-lithographic method. The words 'Printed in Bavaria' or 'Printed in Saxony' can often be seen in the space where the stamp goes on unused examples of such cards.

So, having charted the development of the postcard from its birth to the end of the Victorian era, the next stage is to look at the variety of subjects depicted on these small, rectangular pieces of card; pieces of card that the Edwardians, and later generations, were to become so enthusiastic about.

# Chapter Two

# Views and Places

Postcard collectors could be said to belong to one of two camps. There are the 'subject' collectors — those that look for cards on one particular subject, be it railway, theatre, ships, animals, glamour postcards, or whatever appeals. Then you have the topographical card hunters, looking for cards showing views, town and village scenes, buildings and places of interest, busy streets or country lanes, usually of the country or town where the collector was born, once lived or lives now. These two groups are split fairly evenly with perhaps just *over* half specializing in the 'views and places' category. However, many collectors have more than one collection and will look for cards of their home town as well as their

Morpeth. St. Mary's Church.

CHERTSE

Pier and Sands, Bournemouth

SUTTON POYNTZ Nr WEYMOUTH

favourite subject.

The hunter of topographical postcards will not be disappointed, for previous generations were not slow to capture on film the high street as it then looked, the view from the top of the hill, the pier or the church. However, when looking through a dealer's boxes of view cards (usually sorted by county), the new collector will notice a wide range of prices corresponding to a scale of desirability. At the top of the scale there may be a few cards in the £20/$36 plus bracket and at the opposite end, a number of cards which can be picked up for 50 pence/90 cents or less, with others at practically every price in between. So what makes one particular topographical card worth a hundred times more than another? A look at some of the factors involved may give an idea.

A collector of cards showing the high street of his home town as it was eighty years ago will quickly become familiar with the terms 'real photo' and 'printed photo'. A 'real photo' is literally just that: a postcard produced by a photographic method with a glossy, photograph-like finish, as opposed to one with a printed, usually matt image. When it comes to small towns and village scenes one can generally assume that real photographic cards would have been produced by the local photographer in small numbers, whereas printed photographic cards, which were often coloured, would have been produced in large quantities by a local or national publisher. Therefore the scarcity of the real photo, together with the (more often than not) extra clarity of the image and the

local nature of the cards makes them more desirable and, therefore, more pricey than their printed counterparts.

The next thing to consider is the view itself. The locality of the view depicted will have a great bearing on its price. City centres abound, with streets in central London, Birmingham, Glasgow and other built-up areas in far greater supply than demand. With hundreds of similiar views of Piccadilly Circus or the Strand in the dealers' boxes, and relatively few collectors looking for them, there will always be plenty left at 30-50 pence/50-90 cents. Similarly, owing to the expansion of the railway network

*Below* An alley-way photographed c.1905. Note how the men in the street were curious, but not shy, about the camera.

in Victorian times, it was easy for Edwardian families to travel to the coast and spend their holidays at one of the major seaside resorts. Therefore, the seaside postcard flourished, with coloured views of the seafront, the pier, the promenade and the bandstand produced aplenty to be bought as souvenirs and sent to friends back at home. Views such as these, then, also tend to outnumber the people looking for them, with the result that they can easily be found for around £1/$1.80. This is not to discredit them, of course, and if the collector is interested in these coastal towns with their beaches and bathing machines, piers and

bandstands, then a large and interesting collection could be built up at fairly low cost.

But let us take, for example, a card depicting the road running through a small country village. The card is a real photo, and on one side of the picture you have the village store, with the shopkeeper standing proudly in the doorway, while, in the road, a couple of cyclists are approaching and children play or stand inquisitively looking at the camera. The local photographer captured the scene on film; the view is much more interesting than a simple photograph of an empty street because of the activity going on. Having taken the photograph, he makes up only a handful of postcards to sell locally and, of these, only one or two have survived to the present day. The dozen of so collectors looking for cards of this neighbourhood far outweighs the supply of these superb animated street scenes. No wonder then that prices around £15/$27 can be asked, and paid, for such cards. With the addition of transport, close-ups of motor buses and trams, the prices will be even higher. This is discussed in a later chapter.

A bit of common sense can be used to work out whether a particular view postcard is likely to be plentiful. Most well-known tourist attractions, landmarks and famous buildings would have been well served by the postcard publishers of the day and are therefore likely to be common and of low value. The same can be said of castles, cathedrals, churches and stately homes; a comprehensive collection, containing hundreds and even thousands of such cards, could be put together for the nominal sum of 25-75 pence/40 cents-$1.30 for each card.

CAIRO — Sphinx and the

*Left* Early British 'court-size' view postcard, with room for a message on the picture side.

*Left* One of a series of paintings of Egypt dating from around 1920.

ds

It should be noted that the prices so far mentioned for the topographic cards, especially the good street scenes, are for Edwardian examples. Later cards, including those produced in the 1930s-50s period and even some of the 1960s, are still collectable, but the prices for these cards will be much reduced compared to their earlier counterparts.

Before leaving the British photographic view card, mention should be made of a particular photographer known simply as 'LL'. A Frenchman, whose full name is believed to be Louis Levy, he photographed a great many British and French views, all of which bear the title of the view and the initials 'LL' in the caption. The standard of photography of his cards is generally very high and they interest the local collector as well as those who specialize in his work. Prices currently range between £2-£5/ $3.50-$9, depending on location.

Not every view postcard was necessarily produced from a photograph. A number of extremely good artists flourished during the postcard's golden age and it is well worth tracking down the wide variety of landscapes, woodland scenes, country cottages, picturesque town houses and tranquil seascapes that flowed from their brushes. Some of the best-known and most collectable of these artists include Walter Hayward-Young (who signed his cards 'Jotter'), Alfred Robert Quinton (A.R.Q.), Henry Wimbush, Charles Flower and Van Hier and were backed up by many others, whose output was smaller, and many more unsung artists, whose postcards did not bear their names. An extremely attractive collection can be made either by searching out the works of one or two favourite artists, or collecting the output of one publisher who specialized in this type of card. Raphael Tuck are perhaps the best known of these publishers, with their 'Oilette' range of cards reproducing a superb range of paintings in colour and usually issued in sets of six. Some of them (their 'Oilfacsim' series) were even given a special finish to make them feel like real oil paintings.

*Right* Butcher's shopfront, with staff proudly posing for the camera. Note the meat hanging outside — public health regulations were obviously not as strict in those days. £15/$27 for a card such as this.

# Chapter Three

# Social History

With the social history postcard, we come to a particular type of topographical card which is often the most sought-after by dealers and the most keenly-contested at auction. They are the postcards with that little something extra which makes them more interesting and, therefore, more in demand than the majority of views and run-of-the-mill street scenes. So what exactly falls into the category 'social history postcard'? Briefly, we have those scenes which typify everyday life as it was in previous (in this case, mainly Edwardian) times. We have town and village people going about their day-to-day business and we have those events which would only happen once in a while.

As with the topographical cards previously discussed, the best ones will almost always be the real photographic types. Those depicting the workman carrying out his trade, the blacksmith, the delivery man with his horse-drawn cart or the farmer operating some long-redundant piece of machinery, have a fascination today which appeals to all collectors interested in how we used to live. Couple this with the clarity of the image (in most cases) and the scarcity of this type of card and you have a situation in which demand usually far exceeds supply, with the result that it can be an expensive area in which to start collecting. However, this should not put off the newer collector as one card purchased at £20/$36 can, in the long run, turn out to be a better bargain than twenty cards bought for £1/$1.80 each. Prices for social history material seem always to be on the up, and there are certainly some

superb cards to be found in this interesting category.

Looking at the images themselves, firstly we come to those depicting the Edwardian men and women earning their daily crust. Not such a popular subject in their own time, this may explain why only very small quantities of most were produced, (probably to be sold locally) and why they can be extremely

*Below* Chipping Sodbury sheep sale — superb photographic cards brimming with life do not stay long in the dealer's box. At least £15/$27 per card.

difficult to find in the present day.

The farmer and agricultural worker are well worth tracking down in this category because, of course, farming days, as depicted on the Edwardian postcard, are never to be seen again. It was a labour-intensive business, the farm labourers working long, hard hours for low wages. Even though the petrol-driven tractor had been developed early in the century, it was not until after the First World War that it became commonly used. The result is that there are some superb ploughing, reaping and haymaking scenes to be found on old postcards; often the whole family can be seen with pitchforks, loading hay onto a horse-drawn cart, or the labourer is found guiding the plough behind his team of horses. There are also the sheep-shearing and dipping,

SODBURY SEPTEMBER SHEEP SALE.

woodcutting and crop-picking cards, and those depicting hop-picking scenes, mainly in Kent, where hundreds of people were employed by the hop-farmers for a month or so each autumn to gather in the crop.

Among the other cards showing people at work are those covering the industrial trades. The coal industry was the largest employer of labour and the leading

*Below* Another fine example of a photographic card, showing Retford Market.

contributor to the country's prosperity, with output and numbers of men employed rising steadily during the Edwardian period (although difficult working conditions and failure to install new machinery led to lower productivity per man). Together with the iron, steel and textile industries, coal mining is a popular subject for collectors. Miners and collieries, steelworks, factories and cotton mills can all be found on postcards, in both real and printed-photo form, with the best cards in these categories fetching £12-£15/$22-$27.

There are, of course, many other professions which have been depicted on postcards, and interesting collections can be put together, if a little time is spent on tracking them down. The fishing industry, quarrying, brewing

(close to many people's hearts), lacemaking and medical cards (nurses and ward scenes) are just a few worth looking out for.

As mentioned previously, cards featuring city centres, especially London, are a lot less sought-after than those of smaller towns and villages. One exception to this are those social history cards which were published in various series called 'London Life'. A popular

*Below* A souvenir seaside card showing the Palace Pier at Brighton.

subject among Edwardian publishing companies, over a dozen of them issued cards depicting life and occupations, as witnessed daily in the capital. The most well-known of these series is probably that produced by the Rotary Photographic Company, whose 'London Life' cards were all real photographs, depicting such typical London characters as the chimney sweep, newspaper boy, postman, pavement artist, bootblack, flower seller, Chelsea pensioner and coster with his barrow. Until recently some of the scarcer cards in the series were selling for between £60-£90/$108-$162 each at auction, but prices seem to have settled somewhat and now £50/$90 or so seems to be the ceiling price, with the more plentiful examples starting at about £6-£8/$11-$14. 'London Life'

cards by other publishers tend to be cheaper — some are real photographic cards, others printed photos or the works of artists, with prices starting at around £2/$3.50.

Many of the best social history cards are those depicting occasional events or one-off occurrences. Market day was always a popular event, drawing in crowds from the neighbouring towns and villages; it is certainly worth hunting out cards depicting this busy scene in the market square, often with livestock to be bought and sold featuring in the picture. With these, as with most similar cards, having the location of the event mentioned in the caption will add to the value of the card. Many local photographers would write the location on the negative so that it came out as a white, handwritten caption in the finished postcard. Because most collectors of these cards are interested in a particular region, having the location positively identified makes the card more saleable to collectors of that location. Gipsy encampments, funfairs, village fêtes, ox-roastings, poll-declarations and royal visits will all find ready buyers as subjects in their own right; they will also attract the interest of the topographical collector if the town or village in which the event took place is mentioned on the card.

Other special events such as street parades (usually to celebrate a local or national event) and natural and man-made disasters would have the local photographer out in a flash with his camera. Excluding transport disasters (mentioned in the next chapter), this category includes floods, lightning and storm damage, explosions and fires. A typhoid outbreak in Lincoln, in 1905, is one of the more unusual 'disasters' available, with postcards showing the locals queueing up in the street with their buckets for fresh water.

It must be remembered that the photographer's equipment at the beginning of the century was considerably less sophisticated than today, so that when something dramatic happened locally it could mean him having to carry his bulky camera and photographic plates across fields, pushing past onlookers to get a good view of the event. Then, having taken his photographs, a small number of cards would be made up and sold to the locals. This explains why only one or two examples exist of many of the postcards in this category and why today's collector has to pay a reasonably high price to add them to his collection. In fact, the pricing of social history cards is one of the most difficult areas to gauge accurately. Each card has to be judged on its own merits; the location, the significance of the event, the clarity of the image, the amount of animation (action) in the photograph and the scarcity of cards of that particular event will all have some effect on the price. It is important for the collector to bargain with the dealer, to come to a figure that suits both buyer and seller.

Before leaving the subject of social history, mention should be made of one more category which is popular with collectors. This category is shop fronts. By this I mean postcards showing small village stores and corner shops often with the proud owner standing in the doorway. A wide range of general and speciality shops can be unearthed, with real photographic cards mostly falling into the £5-£15/$9-$27 price range. Of particular interest are the village post-offices and shops with a range of postcards displayed in the windows; these show the postcard-historian how the cards were sold the first time around.

# Chapter Four

# Transport

*Below* A comic card by Tom Browne: a reminder that motoring was not always what it was cracked up to be.

The very general heading of 'Transport' covers an extremely wide variety of postcards which overlap into both the 'topographical' and 'subject' categories. For the sake of simplicity, this chapter has been split into four main sections, each of which has its own avid collectors and each really deserving a chapter to itself to do the subject justice. The four sections, then, are road transport, railways, aviation and shipping.

The Edwardian era was an age of transport revolution, with many of the greatest technological advances of the period occurring within this field. The first two decades of this century saw the slow disappearance of the horse-drawn carriage, but some good photographic cards can be found depicting the typical fully-laden coach and horses, usually photographed outside a hotel or inn before setting off on the day's outing. There are also several high-quality art cards to be found, most notably in the 'Coaching Days' series published by Raphael Tuck, today priced around the £3/$5 mark.

In the transition period between the horsedrawn carriage and the motor carriage bicycling became a popular pastime. Initially quite the thing in society, cycling quickly became more generally accepted, its popularity reflected in the variety of photgraphic, advertising and comic cards

*Right* A superb close up of an early motorbus, with driver and conductor standing alongside £30/$54+.

produced.

However, it is the arrival of the motor vehicle on the postcard that has collectors reaching deep into their wallets and purses. The petrol-driven motor car was initially a luxury item, a plaything for the rich (as exemplified by Toad, in Kenneth Grahame's *Wind in the Willows*), but, by the end of the era, it was accepted as a normal means of transport, with over 130,000 cars in Britain by 1914. With the first death on the roads caused by a petrol-driven vehicle in 1899 and the need to introduce the first speed limit in 1903, not everyone was thrilled by the arrival of the age of the motor car. There were even stories of outraged carriage drivers whipping the motor car driver as he passed! Whether or not this is true, comic postcards can be found depicting the new motor car racing down the high street, animals and people fleeing to get out of its way. Photographic cards depicting close-ups of the Edwardian family car are also worth searching out at about £5-$9 each. Along with the advent of the motor car came motor car racing, another subject eagerly sought by the motoring postcard enthusiast. The Brooklands Racetrack, opened in 1907, was depicted on cards of the time; today these are priced at about £5/$9, upwards. Early racing cars and races (such as the 1903 Gordon-Bennet event) are popular enough to be snapped

up at £10/$18 each.

It is, however, the depiction of public transport that makes up the cream of the crop. The electric tram was initially well-liked during the Edwardian era, the tram did not add to the new problem of exhaust fumes in the streets and had a large carrying capacity (the model introduced by the London County Council in 1907 could hold 78 passengers). Tramline mileage doubled during the first few years of Edward VII's reign. Continued enthusiasm amongst today's collectors ensures healthy prices in this category, where cards tend to be real photographs taken by local photographers and therefore produced in fairly small quantities. They can be found depicting good close up views, track laying, trial trips, opening ceremonies (often captioned 'the first electric tram at . . .') and trams decorated for special events. The best cards can easily command a figure of £30/$54 or even more.

The improving reliability of the motor bus meant that this method of public transport gradually

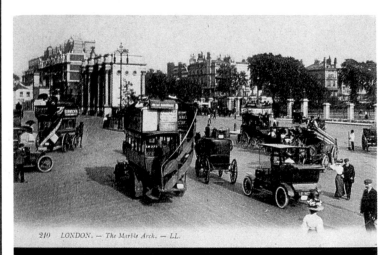

210   LONDON. — The Marble Arch. — LL.

*Below left* Two contrasting road transport postcards. A photograph by 'L.L.' depicting a variety of vehicles at Marble Arch, London. Horse-drawn and motor omnibuses, coach-and-horses, hansom cabs and motor cars can all be seen.

*Below* The Titanic is possibly the most famous ship in the world. Several publishers issued 'In Memoriam' cards after she sank, although many examples actually depict doctored views of her sister ship, the Olympic.

displaced the tram. The first one was introduced in 1905 and three years later there were as many as 1,000 motor buses in London. Horse-drawn cabbies had been known to sneak up side roads so that their passengers would not see how slowly they were going compared with the new buses. As with tram postcards, real photographic close-ups of buses, with the location mentioned in the caption, or the destination clearly visible, will be the subject of spirited competition between the bus/tram collector and the collector of topographic cards of the particular area in question. This usually results in a £30/$54 price tag for many examples, with the best topping the £50/$90 mark. Indeed, auction prices for the top cards frequently exceed £50/$90 and, with the ever-increasing demand, this high figure could be tomorrow's average.

Other methods of motor transport to be found on cards include traction engines, lorries, fire-engines and charabancs. The first three of these are, in general, comparable in scarcity and price to the motor buses. Charabancs are the exception, cards dating from the 1920s being fairly common and usually selling for £2-£3/$3.50—$5.

Leaving the busy Edwardian streets, with their horse-drawn omnibuses, motor buses, trams, hansom cabs and motor cars, we come to another popular area amongst today's collectors — the railway. Being the standard method of travelling any kind of distance, until the motor car became more widely owned by the masses, most aspects of the railway have been well-covered by postcard publishers. The large numbers of cards depicting close-up views of locomotives offer the new collector a subject in which a

*Above* A fine study of a motor bus run by the Great Eastern Railway. Railway companies would often run bus services in areas where branch lines were not justified.

sizeable collection can be put together without too much outlay — maybe a pound or two per card, although albums of such cards can be bought at auction with the price working out at less than £1/$1.80 each. Raphael Tuck produced a number of sets in the 'Oilette' range, depicting art views of railway engines, and the Locomotive Publishing Company produced many close-up photographic views.

There was much competition between the various railway companies to attract the attention of the traveller; the postcard was used as a means of publicity. Both before and after the 1923 grouping companies produced cards showing engines, carriages and landmarks on the line, to promote

their particular firm. These 'railway official' cards as they are called, were most prolifically issued by the London and North Western Railway, and usually sell for £1-£2/$1.80-$3.50 each. Cards can also be found showing ships and hotels owned and used by the larger companies; these are usually in the £3-£6/$5-$11 price bracket. The most expensive of these 'officials' are the colour cards reproducing advertising posters, the best of which change hands for £40-£60/$72-$108, and early vignette views produced by minor railway companies, at £20/ $36 or so. With the ever-increasing traffic on the roads, the underground electric railway was gaining in popularity. Cards depicting the District and

Metropolitan railway form a sought-after 'branch line' for the London/railway collector.

But of all the various railway postcards, the ones probably most in demand are those depicting railway stations. Here again, as with many of the motor transport and social history cards, the 'subject' and 'topographical' categories overlap. Real photographic cards depicting interior views of country stations, with the station-master and passengers in evidence, are not at all common and are keenly hunted by the collector of the town or village in which it is situated, as well as by the railway station specialist. Therefore, prices can easily go to £20/$36 for the best cards, although, in view of their quality and the demand for such cards, this may soon be considered cheap and perhaps a £50/$90 average is not too far away. The big city stations are, however, more plentiful and fetch a fraction of the price of their village counterparts — usually around £1.50-£2/$3-$3.50 each.

Moving on to aviation, we have another subject in which certain cards (namely early meetings, with the locality mentioned on the card) are popular with topographic collectors as well. Postcard publishers were not slow to cover the achievements of Blériot when he became the first to cross the English Channel by plane, ('Britain is no longer an Island' said the newspapers), and since then civil and military aircraft of all types have appeared on postcards in their day. Cards depicting gatherings of early aircraft and their pilots at meetings, c. 1909/1910, often with crowds of onlookers, will fetch upwards of £12/$22 and are amongst the top-valued cards in this category. (This is ignoring

*Right* Early aviators and their machines are popular with collectors. These three examples are from the 'Flying at Hendon' series.

certain 'flown' cards with additional postmark interest). Well worth looking out for, too, are cards in the series entitled 'Flying At Hendon', which are real photographs of pilots with their machines and are good value at an average of £6-£8/$11-$14.

Early aeroplanes were also depicted in art form by the publishers Raphael Tuck, again in several series of their 'Oilette' range, as were airships — a subsection of the aviation category which has a strong following. It should be noted, however, that, although most photographic cards of airships would fetch upwards of £5/$9, those depicting Zeppelins apparently being shot down at night (often with coloured flames) are common and are only worth a pound or two.

The subject of shipping or maritime postcards is a complex one. Like the railway companies, the various shipping companies would issue advertising cards to publicize their services, but,

130.H.P. BREGUET WARPLANE. FLYING AT HENDON.

MR W.T. WARREN. CAUDRON BIPLANE. FLYING AT HENDON.

FLYING AT HENDON. MESSRS M. DESOUTTER & G.W. BEATTY.

because of the extremely large numbers involved (over 300 shipping lines worldwide have produced cards), of varying scarcity value, the beginner should proceed with caution. The best of the poster-type adverts will fetch at least £20/$36, but cards depicting the ships themselves can be priced at anything from £1/$1.80 upwards, depending on the ship (some were in service for years, whilst others sank on their maiden voyage). Of course, the most famous of maiden voyage disasters was that of the Titanic. Popularity here keeps prices up, with the various 'In Memoriam' Cards produced after sinking making between £15-£30/$27–$54, depending on the publisher. Photographic pre-sinking cards are similarly priced, with general art and post-sinking photographic views considered of less value (many such cards actually being doctored views of the Titanic's sister ship, the Olympic). As well as producing railway and aviation themes Raphael Tuck produced a range of shipping cards, with many 'Oilettes' of famous liners. This particular subject also has many sub-themes for the collector to explore; these include ferries and pleasure boats, sailing ships, lifeboats (very popular), ships' interiors, harbours and docks and shipyards (by 1914, 60 per cent of the world's ships were being built in British yards, with Southampton

WRECK OF THE LEEDS & NEWCASTLE EXP
5893. G.

shipyard probably the most sought-after from the postcard point of view).

To round off the transport section, there is a category which links motor transport, railways, aviation, shipping, topographical and social history: the category can be termed the accident, wreck or disaster theme. The motor accident, train crash or shipwreck would immediately send local photographers to the scene to record the incident, and cards were often produced for sale within a day or two. Today the keen demand from 'subject' and topographic collectors ensures that these cards are valued at the top end of their particular categories, with a rough price guide of £6-£15/$11-$27 for most railway, aviation and shipping disasters. Motor bus/tram/traction engine crashes fetch upwards of £20-£30/$36-$54 if they are clear, real photographic close-ups. One publisher in this category deserves a mention: Warner Gothard of Barnsley specialized in producing photograpic, composite pictures (or montages) of national events and disasters. Their output covered boiler explosions and colliery fires, as well as railway accidents, ship collisions and a tram disaster. Warner Gothard postcards are well worth looking out for; prices for the most common start at just under £20/$36, rising to about £60/$108 for the rarest examples.

*Left* Local photographers were quick to capture unusual events that happened in their area, such as this spectacular train crash of 1907.

# Chapter Five

# Glamour, Art Nouveau and Art Deco

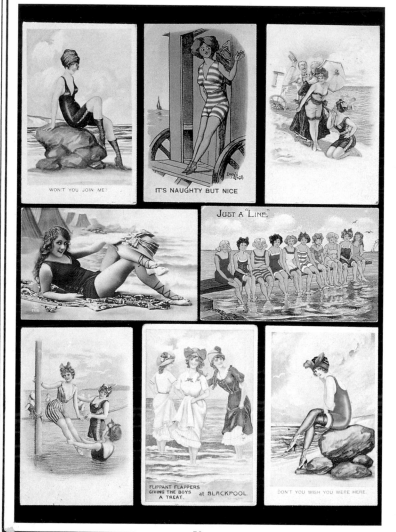

WON'T YOU JOIN ME?

IT'S NAUGHTY BUT NICE

JUST A "LINE"

FLIPPANT FLAPPERS
GIVING THE BOYS
A TREAT.     at BLACKPOOL.

DON'T YOU WISH YOU WERE HERE.

Moving away from postcards which have topographical connections, we come to one of the most popular subject categories. The term 'glamour' covers all pretty girls depicted on picture postcards, from the head-and-shoulders study of the American beauty to the lingerie-clad young thing in her Parisian boudoir, from the chromolithographic depiction of the finely-dressed society lady to the photographic studio portrait of the nude. Possibly because the great majority of postcard artists and photographers were male, pretty girls far outnumber handsome young men in their work. Yet, despite the fact that glamour cards in all their forms are fairly plentiful, there remains a large band of collectors looking for them and, at auction, there are

*Far left* Bathing beauties make an interesting and colourful collection within the 'glamour' category. However, costumes such as these were generally found only on the artist's canvas and in the photographer's studio, and were not commonly worn on the beaches in those days!

*Below* A small sample of the work of Raphael Kirchner, probably the most collected of all glamour artists.

often more bids received for these cards than any other subject.

Any new postcard collector is bound to come across the name Raphael Kirchner before too long. Probably the most famous of all the glamour artists, his cards fetch a premium over and above the prices made by similar cards by other artists. Born in Vienna, in 1876, his early cards by European publishers currently make £20-£40/$36-$72, with a few scarcer designs nearer £60/$108. Cards published in France, following his move to that country, are more plentiful and sell for £12-£20/$22-$36, with British issues put out around the time of the First World War (such as the Bruton Galleries series) making £8-£12/$14-$22. Kirchner's cards were usually issued in series, each with a theme such as 'Sunrays', 'Marionettes', *'Enfants de la Mer'* (bathing), 'The Mikado' and 'The Geisha' (Japanese girls), 'Seven Deadly Sins', 'Cycling', *'Les Parfums'* and *'Fruits Douces'*, often in the Art Nouveau style. The collector may also notice that all the pretty girls depicted on Kirchner's cards have similar faces — explained by the fact that he used his very beautiful wife Nina as his model. One such card is entitled *'Lelie Fumeuse d'Opium'*, slightly prophetic as Nina did indeed take to drugs and later died in a mental institution.

Other artists whose cards were produced in Paris during the Edwardian period and whose output in terms of quality was on a par with Kirchner include Maurice Millière, Suzanne Meunier, Maurice Pépin, Hérouard, Penot, Léonnec, Fontan, Fabiano and Ney. All specializing in drawing girls in various states of undress, their cards usually come in sets of five, six or seven and today fetch between £5-£8/$9-$14 per card

(£25-£55/$45-$99 per set). Certainly worth looking out for, these prices can be considered cheap when compared to the Kirchner cards; perhaps many collectors, who feel the latter are too expensive, will turn more to the work of other glamour artists, pushing prices up all round.

Italian artists from the Edwardian to the 1920s era were responsible for producing a good crop of glamour postcards which generally tend to be a little cheaper than the French ones mentioned above (except, that is, for the Art Deco types). Nanni, Mauzan, Corbella, Colombo, Cherubini, Bertiglia and Busi are the names often found under the chic fashion, head-and-shoulders and romantic portraits put out by the Italian postcard publishers. Again, often in sets of six, they seem good value at between £3/$5 and £6/$11 per card, although the more colourful Art Deco examples would probably make double these prices.

Slightly different in style yet again, and perhaps more in demand in the United States, is the work of the glamour artists from the North American continent. To the forefront here we have Phillip Boileau and Harrison Fisher, whose subjects tend to be finely-dressed, sophisticated women, active all-American girls out punting and driving, or the speculative beauty, drawn in head-and-shoulders close up. Many series of supposedly typical portraits of American girls were issued; one example is simply entitled 'The American Girl' by Alice Luella Fidler and Pearl Fidler LeMunyon (two of the few female artists working in this category) and runs to over 130 cards. An interesting collection by American artists such as these can be formed for around £2-£4/$3.50-

$7 per card and might also include the work of Charles Dana Gibson, whose Edwardian creation 'The Gibson Girl' is typified on many of his cards.

Photographic postcards depicting nudes tend to be the product of French studios and would have been imported into this country for sale 'underground', perhaps in gentlemen's clubs or obtainable by mail order. Sometimes the nude models were shown in rather coy poses, others were more openly erotic, whilst sets of six cards can be found in which the model disrobes in her boudoir, wearing a little less in each successive card. However, the photographic nude was not as publicly acceptable as her artist-drawn sister and would not have been displayed in the corner shops, hotels and railway stations alongside the thousands of other postcards for sale. It would also be extremely difficult to find one postally-used, as the Post Office would almost certainly have confiscated anything of this nature if posted, (and the postman may well have slipped such a card into his pocket if it got as far as him!). These unknown models, photographed by photographers who remained anonymous in order to avoid prosecution, are keenly sought-after today, fetching £4-£6/$7-$11 each; this price could soon be set for a considerable rise as this already popular subject attracts more new collectors.

The Art Nouveau field is dominated by one man — Alphonse Mucha. A Czechoslovakian artist, he achieved great success during the 1890s as a poster-designer and book illustrator, his work including the much-applauded posters of Sarah Bernhardt and 'Job' cigarette-paper advertisements

*Below* Four examples of Italian Art Deco, including
one by Achille Mauzan (top right), two by Tito
Corbella (below), and an unsigned design.
Reasonably priced at up to £6/$11.

*Right* A highly desirable set of Art Nouveau
designs by the Belgian artist Henri Meunier.
£500-£800/$900-$1,440.

*Bottom* Two of the author's favourite postcards,
from Meissner & Buch of Leipzig, Germany,
publishers of many extremely fine designs.

(both of which have been reproduced on postcards). In fact many of his flowing designs of flower-adorned young maidens were made available in postcard form; today they are highly prized and very rare. Usually turning up at auction, the cheapest Mucha cards start at around £20/$36, but £40-£80/$72-$144 is a more usual price. The scarcest of designs can easily top even this and, when a fine collection of Art Nouveau and glamour postcards was auctioned at Phillips in February 1988, certain examples by Mucha made over £200/$360 each. Some of Mucha's contemporaries, whose superb Art Nouveau postcards make £30-£70/$54-$126, include Henri Meunier, Arpad Basch, E. Docker, Nini Hager and Elizabeth Sonrel. Certainly, I feel that some of the most beautiful cards ever published come under the Art Nouveau heading, but it remains one of the most expensive areas in which to start collecting.

Likewise, Art Deco has its dedicated followers searching for the work of its leading exponents. Highly-stylized floral themes, geometric patterns and vivid colours can all be found on these cards of the post-First World War era. In the Phillips auction mentioned above, a set of six cards by the Italian Deco artist, Brunelleschi, sold for just over £500/$900 and four by Montedoro fetched £200/$360, but the new collector interested in starting a collection in this subject need not necessarily pay such high prices. It is possible to pick up good examples by some of the lesser-rated artists for about £5-£10/$9-$18 and it is also worth looking out for unsigned cards. Some extremely attractive Art Nouveau and Deco cards can be found bearing no signature; these anonymous designs change hands

*Below* A photographic postcard of a nude. Like so
many of this type, the card was produced in Paris.

*Below* Four superb unsigned Art Nouveau designs. The bottom two, published by Raphael Tuck, are almost certainly by the artist Eva Daniell, and are rated at £40/$72 each.

*Right* A real photographic card of an Egyptian glamour girl *c.* 1920!

*Below right* 'The American Girl', as interpreted by Canadian artist Philip Boileau.

NATIVE WOMAN, CAIRO. NO. 19.

A MISCHIEFMAKER.

LITTLE LADY DEMURE.

for anything between £2-£12/ $3.50-$22, the exact price depending on the particular merits of the card in question.

Even more expensive than the best Art Nouveau and Deco postcards can be those that come from the various classic series, published on the continent around the turn of the century. Turning up very infrequently these days and usually at auction when they do, these series include the work of many of the great artists of the period, including the likes of Mucha, although not necessarily in the 'glamour' or Art Nouveau style. Mostly priced from £30/$54 per card (with the scarcest fetching upwards of £300/$540), the new collector is not likely to come across many examples. They are, in fact, more in demand in Europe than in Britain.

*Right* This risqué 1902 card is not in fact a photograph from life but a reproduction of a painting and is therefore of little value.

*Below* Six of a set of 12 'Months of the Year' by Alphonse Mucha. Value for complete set £600-£900/ $1,080-$1,620.

However, cards to look out for are those bearing the series titles *Collection Des Cent, Wiener Werkstatte, Cocorico, Concours Byrrh, Maîtres de la Carte Postale* and *Editions Cinos.* As with all 'glamour', Art Nouveau and Art Deco cards, exactly what you collect is really a matter of personal taste — I am sure that many collectors actually prefer the £3-£5/$5-$9 cards to those ten times that price.

As a footnote to this section it is important to add that collectors interested in looking out for other works by many of these 'glamour' artists, should keep their eyes open for French magazines produced in the 1890-1920 period. Publications such as *La Vie Parisienne* often had full-page colour illustrations by the same artists whose works grace many a postcard album page and complement a collection so well.

# Chapter Six

# Entertainment

MR GEORGE EDWARDES'
COMPANY

*Below* Advertising cards were sold to publicise new plays at London and provincial theatres. Very collectable today, most sell for between £6-£12/$11-$22, although examples by some artists, such as this one by W. Barribal, may fetch a little more.

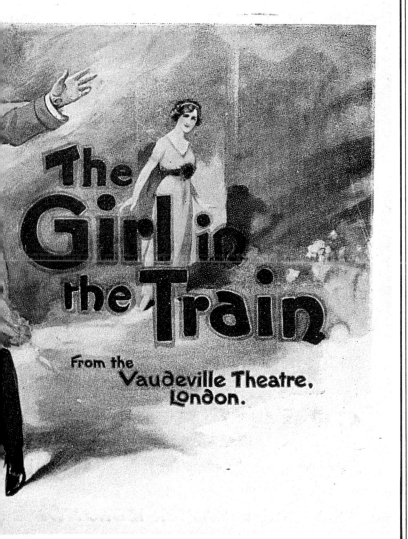

*Below* A selection of leading ladies from the Edwardian stage. Postcards of actresses such as these were produced and sold in their thousands.

*Far right* Most Edwardian actors and actresses seemed more than happy to give their autographs, judging by the numbers of signed cards still to be found. There were even postcards showing them signing other postcards!

Going to the theatre, cinema or sportsground have always been popular leisure pursuits. The large numbers of postcards, depicting every aspect of these activities, reflect this.

The theatrical postcard offers the new collector a means of putting together a reasonable

collection fairly cheaply, with the option of specializing and purchasing the more expensive cards at a later date. Although we may think that the age of the 'superstar' has only been with us since the golden days of Hollywood, many Edwardian actresses were household names and had a huge following. Without the help of television, radio or the silver screen the faces of the most popular were projected into almost every household in the land by means of the picture postcard. It would seem that most of the leading actresses spent more time in the photographic studio than

4122 A  ROTARY PHOTO. E.C  MISS PHYLLIS DARE.  FOULSHAM & BANFIELD

they did on the stage, to judge by the hundreds of thousands of portraits put out by publishing companies such as Rotary, Beagles, Rapid and Philco, who specialized in this field. Almost every Edwardian album would include cards of Marie Studholme, Zena and Phyllis Dare, Gertie Millar, Gabrielle Ray, Mabel Love, Gladys Cooper and Lily Elsie, together with any number of the hundreds of other stars of the stage so adored by the public in this pre-First World War era. The above-named actresses appeared, in the main, in musical comedies, the most popular form of theatrical entertainment of the time. However, devotees of drama were not forgotten and plenty of portraits of the leading lights can still be found; these include such greats as Henry Irving, Ellen Terry and H. B. Tree. But the musical comedy beauties won the day by the sheer number of cards produced (I have heard of one collector who has over 2,000 different cards of Marie

CENTRAL NEWS    GEORGES CARPENTIER.    160 L.
BEAGLES POSTCARDS
FAMOUS BOXERS SERIES

Studholme alone) and the quantity of cards still extant makes these fairly easy to obtain at 30-50 pence/50-90 cents each. Autographed cards are also worth looking out for. Although an autograph collection can encompass politicians, writers, musicians and sportsmen, the Edwardian thespian seems to have been particularly approachable when a signature was wanted. This has resulted in a plethora of signed cards of most actors and actresses of that period

and prices today reflect this, starting from as little as £2/$3.50 a piece. Moving up the price range a little, the collector can add to his collection by including some of the fine poster-type advertising cards available. Publishers such as David Allen produced many of the large colour posters (often drawn by leading artists of the day), used to publicize particular plays; these posters were often reproduced in postcard form. They can make up an interesting collection in themselves and are well worth picking up at £5-£12/$9-$22 each, the higher prices being for those by the most favoured artists.

Briefly leaving behind the Edwardian era and jumping forward a couple of decades, we find the star of the screen replacing the star of the stage in the postcard-buying public's affections. Not produced in such large numbers as their earlier counterparts, the market for photographic portraits of cinema celebrities from the 1920s to the 1950s is today fairly strong, although it would be true to say that only certain 'big names' are in demand. Laurel and Hardy, Marilyn Monroe, Marlene Dietrich, Shirley Temple, John Wayne and Greta Garbo fall into this latter group, selling at around £3-£5/$5-$9, with the majority of other film star portraits priced at

*Left* Photographic portraits of sportsmen have always been keenly sought, with cricketers, golfers, boxers, footballers and tennis players leading the field at between £4 and £12/$7 and $22 each.

*Below* Seaside holiday entertainment was often provided by concert parties such as the troupe of pierrots and pierrettes depicted on this privately-produced postcard.

*Far right* Harold Lloyd, one of the silent screen's great comedians, and Jobyna Ralston, the leading lady in his six films between 1923 and 1927. Around £2-£4/$3.50-$7 would be the price for cards such as these.

The Olympian Concert Party, Eastbourne. 1917.

£1-£3/$1.80-$5.

There are so many other avenues open to the performing arts collector that they can only be mentioned in passing. Suffice to say that fans of opera, classical music, ballet, circus and music hall will not be disappointed with the output of the postcard publisher of the past, and everything from pierrots to Pavlova, magicians to Mozart can be found by looking carefully through the dealers' albums.

Though women dominated the performing arts (especially from the postcard point of view), the female influence in sport, at the turn of the century, was almost non-existent. Cricket and football were then, as now, the chief summer and winter sports and their continuing popularity has always resulted in a strong demand for cards depicting teams and individual players. Several publishers issued series showing the famous and not-so-famous exponents of these sports. These change hands today for £5-£10/$9-$18 per card. Golf is another very

popular sport whose players (in postcard form) fall into the same price range; hot on the heels of these 'big three' come boxing and horse-racing. The publisher Beagles produced a comprehensive selection of real photographic cards in their 'Famous Boxers' series (£3-£5/$5-$9 each), whilst horse-racing, a sport which crossed all class barriers in its appeal, was further popularized by royal patronage (Edward VII was a racehorse-owner and regular race-goer). A variety of horses, jockeys, courses and colours can be found on contemporary postcards at around £2-£5/$3.50-$9 each.

As well as the host of other sports and games to be found by the keen collector, Edwardian hobbies and crazes were depicted on postcards. Playing diabolo and rinking (roller-skating on a purpose-built rink) are just two that may be set for a revival as the number of collectors grow — but then again, perhaps just collecting the cards is strenuous enough for some!

HAROLD LLOYD.

JOBYNA RALSTON

# Chapter Seven

# The Best of the Rest

From advertising to animals, exhibitions to exploration, royalty to romance, any subject one cares to mention has almost certainly been depicted on the picture postcard at one time or another. In this chapter the intention is to take a brief look at just a few of the many other types of card available, hopefully providing the reader with a few ideas as to what to collect himself.

For the early Edwardians war was something that happened to other people in other places — a view that was to change quite dramatically by the end of 1918. The Boer war coincided with the beginning of the postcard craze and was a popular subject with the publishers of the day. Patriotic cards in Britain and anti-British cartoons and caricatures in Europe sold extremely well and, from the turn of the century onwards, portraits of the great military leaders started appearing in the shops. There were artists who specialized in painting military scenes and their work is very collectable today; in Britain Harry Payne is much in demand, whilst continental artists such as Becker and Schonpflug have a steady following. The styles range from high-quality studies of soldiers wearing the uniforms of named regiments, through to vignette views of regiments in action and caricatures making fun of army types. The 1914-18 war kept publishers very busy satisfying the demands of the postcard-buying public, a fact that explains the large numbers of cards from that period still available today. Pro-recruitment cards and patriotic battle scenes published by the *Daily Mail*, comic cards, machines of war, such as tanks, battleships and submarines, French and Belgian towns before and after bomb damage — all are readily available and most are still very moderately priced (the French/Belgian bomb-damage cards were made in such numbers that they can still be picked up for a few pence each).

*Right* Tom Browne was a popular and fairly prolific comic artist of the Edwardian period. A set of six cards such as this would now cost around £15/$27.

Another product of the first world war was the embroidered silk postcard, used by soldiers at the front to send sentimental messages and greetings to their loved ones back home. Again produced in fairly large numbers (and almost always kept and treasured by the recipient), they are not uncommon today, with prices starting at about £1.50/$3 each. Earlier, scarcer and more expensive are their sister cards made from woven silks. Machine-made in England by the companies of Thomas Steven and W. H. Grant, and also several firms in mainland Europe, these woven examples depicting ships, famous people, exhibitions and 'hands across the sea' are likely to cost the collector a minimum of £15/$27 per card.

Working with young children and animals is something that a postcard cataloguer has to do regularly. A number of postcard artists, whose work crops up fairly often and is keenly collected, specialized in one or other of these two subjects. Taking children first, possibly the most famous artist is Mabel Lucie Attwell, whose chubby little boys and girls appeared over several decades and often reflected the fashions of the day. The new collector will also encounter the work of other nursery artists such as Agnes Richardson, Millicent Sowerby, Ida Outhwaite and Ethel Parkinson (to name but a very

few), as well as the cricket-playing boys of E. P. Kinsella, the nursery rhymes of Randolph Caldicott and the adventures of Golliwog as depicted by Florence Upton. Several artists of the 1920s and '30s painted fairies and elves, often with an Art Deco flavour so typical of the period; these are becoming very collectable now; Margaret Tarrant and Rene Cloke are just two artists to look out for in this field. However, the most expensive of the nursery artists are those whose depictions of children, nursery rhymes and fairies typify the Art Deco style. The superb designs of Joyce Mercer are pehaps the best examples (a set of six of her cards will sell for between £40-£50/$72-

*Below* One of a series of comedy cards by Harry Parlett. Another example can be seen on page 90.

" *Just like the Ivy I'll cling to "you"* "

SONGS
Illustrated

$90; charming collections can be made of other favourites, such as C. E. Shand, Hilda T. Miller and the Dutch artist Henriette Willebeek Le Mair, whose pastel watercolours usually come in sets of twelve with titles such as 'Our Old Nursery Rhymes' and 'Little Songs of Long Ago'.

Mention artists who specialized in drawing animals and the first name to spring to a postcard collector's mind would almost certainly be that of Louis Wain.

*Below and right* Two of a series of children's cards by Rene Cloke. These are now becoming increasingly popular and are valued at £2/$3.60 each.

HER GAYEST PAINTS
THIS FAIRY BRINGS
TO TINT THE
"PAINTED LADY'S" WINGS.

Although he did occasionally draw dogs, pigs and birds Wain is really regarded as being *the* cat man. From the first appearance of his sketches of cats in the newspapers of the 1880s his popularity was assured; the hundreds of his designs which came out in postcard form helped spread his fame across the nation. He drew portraits of such cats as the 'Russian Blue', the 'Orange Persian', the 'Brown Tabby' and 'Lucky Black Cat', and produced a series called 'At the Cat Show'. But perhaps more popular are his many comical anthropomorphic designs (that is, representations of partly-dressed cats in human situations). In this category there are scenes like 'The Busy Fluffkin Family Moving House' (a chaotic furniture-removal scene). 'A Cat's Matrimony' (a comic wedding scene), 'Who Shaid Ppussshy Foot? (a drunken cat!), 'The Morning Bath' and 'Preparing for the Party'; cats are shown involved

AN ELFIN SERENADE.

*Below* Practically every subject imaginable was depicted on the Edwardian comic postcard. Scouting and political comics are two of the most collected areas today.

*Right* One of a set of six superb designs by Louis Wain, which sold for £95/$171 at a Phillips auction in 1988.

in various activities, from playing diabolo to theatre-going and playing a range of roles, from Santa Claus to 'Jack the giant-killer'. There is great demand for these cards, so most will cost £10-£20/$18-$36 each. A few scarcer designs, such as those advertising a particular product, may even fetch a little more (there is one very appropriate card advertising the Drury Lane pantomime: *Puss in Boots*).

A list of other animal artists worth mentioning would certainly include Arthur Thiele, whose anthropomorphic cats are not as prolific as those by Louis Wain, but

*Below* Shown at the top is a card from the long military series 'History and Traditions', published by Gale and Polden. The other two cards are examples of the fine military artwork of Harry Payne.

*Right* A selection of First World War embroidered silks. Regimental crests (centre row, left and right) are scarcer and more desirable than the patriotic, sentimental and greetings types.

### 7th (QUEEN'S OWN) HUSSARS.
#### BATTLE HONOURS.
The letters "Q.O." interlaced within the Garter.

"Dettingen,"              "Peninsula"
"Warburg,"                "Waterloo,"
"Beaumont,"               "Lucknow,"
"Williems,"               "South Africa,
"Orthes,"                   1901-02."

#### HISTORY AND TRADITIONS.

The regiment was raised in 1689 in Scotland. In 1694 it proceeded to Flanders and was engaged at Mooreslede, and at the famous siege of Namur. It served in the campaign in Germany, 1710-12. It went to Flanders, 1742-5, and fought at Dettingen, Fontenoy, Roucoux, Lauffeldt, &c. It served in Germany 1760-3, and was present at Warburg and Wilhelmsthal. It went to Flanders again in 1793-5 and fought at Valenciennes, Cateau and several other engagements. In 1799 it was again employed and won much distinction in the short campaign in Holland. In 1808 it went to Spain and took part in the actions at Sahagun, Corion, Benevente and Corunna. In 1813 it returned to the Peninsula and was present at the passage of the Bidassoa, at Orthez and Toulouse. It fought at Waterloo and suffered severely in its many contests with the French Cuirassiers. It was employed in Canada during the insurrection of 1838-9. During the Indian Mutiny it took part in the Relief of Lucknow and in the subsequent campaigns in Oude and the Trans-Gogra, particularly distinguishing itself at the passage of the Betwa. In 1896 it took part in the campaigns in Rhodesia and played a conspicuous part in the later operations in Mashonaland. It served during the South African War and took a gallant share in that arduous campaign.

ARGYLL & SUTHERLAND HIGHLANDERS

*Piper.* Full uniform.

THE BADGES AND THE WEARER
THE ROYAL ARTILLERY

are now catching up in popularity; Lawson Wood with his creation 'Gran'pop the chimpanzee' and George Studdy with his cheeky, cuddly puppy named Bonzo are also popular. Of course, not all animal artists were busy with comic creations. There are many fine cards to be found reproducing life-like paintings, perhaps most often of horses and dogs, with Raphael Tuck to the fore, publishing such cards in their 'Oilette' range. Domestic pets and farm animals, as well as appearing on canvas, regularly found themselves in front of the Edwardian photographer's lens, to judge by the large numbers of cute cats and cuddly dogs to be found on old postcards. Easter bunnies, donkeys, cows, fish and birds, together with lions, tigers and polar bears from Regent's Park and other zoos, were not forgotten either. Generally, though, these photographic animals are less in demand and are therefore cheaper than their artist-drawn cousins, although certain examples, such as named breeds of dogs, sell well. Certainly this whole field is one worthy of consideration by all prospective collectors, although it is perhaps especially appealing to the young as, for a relatively small outlay, an attractive collection can be built up.

The same can be said of the

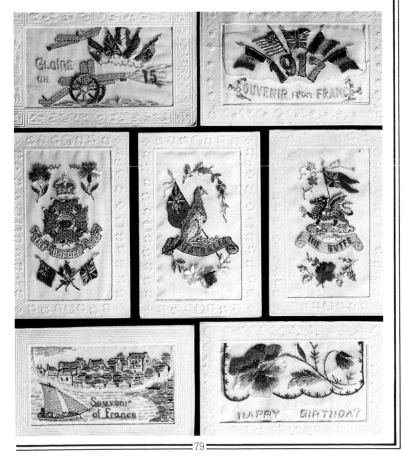

*Left* An example of the wide variety of glossy deckle-edged birthday cards which can still be bought for as little as 25 pence/45 cents.

millions of many different types of Edwardian greetings postcards, which, with a few exceptions, are not so keenly collected today. Cards for Christmas, Easter, birthdays, St. Valentine's day and Thanksgiving, cards depicting letters of the alphabet or the recipient's name spelled out in large letters, New Year cards showing the date made up of snowmen, and calendar cards: all can be found in the dealers' boxes, mostly for modest sums. Earlier cards with embossing and gilding are most sought-after, some of the best examples being found under the Christmas heading. Santa Claus sells steadily, especially on the American market, while snowmen, Christmas angels and the better cards depicting children and snow scenes are good value at around £2-£3/$3.50-$5. On the other hand, the glossy, deckle-edged birthday cards of the 1920s and 1930s can still be bought for as little as 25 pence/45 cents each. Perhaps the most interesting and unusual are the hold-to-light greetings postcards, often depicting wintry scenes and cottages in the snow. The designs incorporate many little coloured cut-out 'windows' which glow when the card is held up to a bright light, perhaps changing the appearance of the picture from a daytime scene to a view at night, with all the lights on inside the cottage. These sell for around £6/$11. However, combine the attractive effect of hold-to-light cards with the popularity of Santa Claus and you have the crème-de-la-crème of the greetings postcard — the 'hold-to-light Santa'. These rare cards occasionally turn up at auction and sell for up to £60/$108 each!

Hold-to-light cards such as these fall into one of my own favourite categories — that of the

*Below* Three good examples of mechanical novelty cards. The lighthouse is a kaleidoscope card, with the beams of light changing colour as the wheel is turned. The others are 'spankers'; gently pulling a lever raises and lowers the hand up from the card and down again. Two cards are pictured in the interests of sexual equality!

novelty postcard. After the initial craze for the postcard had swept the country (and the world) the publishers were always trying to invent new ways to catch the imagination of the public and maintain sales at the same time. This resulted in a variety of unusual ideas being put into production, some clever and attractive, others not much better than mere gimmicks. Some of the best are the 'mechanical' types, the cards with moving parts which actually do something. These include kaleidoscopes with revolving wheels of changing colours, cards such as 'spankers', with parts which move when a lever is pulled and those which open to reveal crêpe-paper chains. There are jigsaw puzzle postcards and even a series which actually had a gramophone record impressed onto the card, which could play a tune at 78 r.p.m. Then we have the cut-out models, such as Tuck's 'Dressing Dolls' series, which have a design ready for cutting-out and making up. Postcards were made from aluminium, leather, wood and celluloid; some had additional materials applied to the picture:

*Below* Children on postcards come in a wide variety of shapes and sizes; the work of most artists specializing in this field has a strong following.

Sweet things and pretty things * * all for your Birthday *

"Now I expect he'll grow."

I'se so lonely Come Soon !

To My Valentine

HRISTCHURCH RD., LONDON, S.W.2

NEW DONALD McGILL COMICS

PRINTED IN GREAT BRITAIN

The war is won, your £. s. d.
Has helped to bring us victory,
But saving still will pave the way
To that new world, for which we pray.

*" KEEP SAVING FOR A RAINY DAY "*

This is a
genuine
**New**
Donald McGill
Comic.

# DO IT NOW

pictures of birds with real stuck-on feathers and pretty girls with real hair! Because many of these novelty cards were made to be played with, they can be fairly difficult to find in perfect working order today and are therefore quite expensive. The appliqué cards may start at only £2/$3.50 or so, but the kaleidoscopes and cut-out models can fetch £30/$54 or more. However, they are amongst the most fascinating of all the subjects to collect.

No book on postcards, no matter how general, would be complete without mention of that staple fare of the postcard-sender: the comic postcard. Very popular with the Edwardians, they are fairly neglected in the current market, except for certain themes and artists; they represent an excellent opportunity for the new collector to accumulate an interesting and varied collection. Everyone knows of the saucy seaside postcards with fat ladies, flirtatious young girls and hen-pecked husbands (as drawn by Donald McGill); indeed, though such cards were one of the few types to remain popular after 1918 they are not in much demand today. Comic illustrators got a lot of mileage out of segregated bathing huts, drunks and the fashions of the day as subject-matter for their postcards; most of these can still be picked up for less than £1/$1.80. More sought-after, however, are comic, political cards. Prime ministers and other political leaders have always been a target for the artist's brush; Asquith, Lord Rosebery and Joseph Chamberlain and the tariff reform/free trade argument of 1903 were no exception. The suffragette movement also provoked a certain amount of disapproval via the picture postcard, and examples on this

*Left* Donald McGill cards are the only comic cards which remained popular after the First World War and originals are highly sought-after. If the card is a reproduction, as in this case, it will be printed with the words 'This is a genuine *New* Donald McGill Comic' and is consequently valueless.

*Below* King Edward VII having a nice cup of tea. This card would appeal to two groups of collectors, as it combines the themes of royalty and advertising.

*Below* Naughty but nice — cleverly-drawn 'fantasy' cards such as this are rare. Such an example should fetch at least £15/$27.

*Below* Four early military cards commemorating the
end of the Boer war, 31st May 1902.

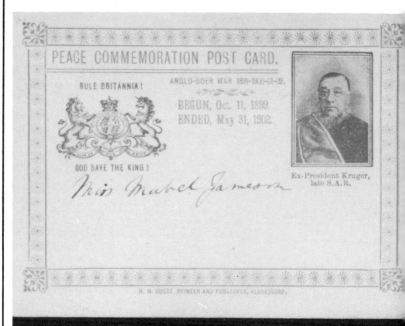

PEACE COMMEMORATION POST CARD.

RULE BRITANNIA!

ANGLO-BOER WAR 1899-1900-01-02.

BEGUN, Oct. 11, 1899.
ENDED, May 31, 1902.

GOD SAVE THE KING!

Ex-President Steyn,
late O.F.S.

H. M. GUEST, PRINTER AND PUBLISHER, KLERKSDORP.

PEACE COMMEMORATION
POST CARD.

ANGLO-BOER WAR 1899-1900-91-02.
BEGUN OCT 11, 1899.
ENDED MAY 31, 1902.

GOD SAVE THE KING!

LOUIS BOTHA, ex-Comdt.-Gen. late S.A.R. (left)
SCHALK BURGER, ex-Acting President do. (right)
Taken at Peace Conference, Klerksdorp, May, '02

*Left  and below* A selection of postcards which can still be bought fairly cheaply. The embossed and gilded Santa Claus card being especially popular. The soldier is one of a series of six cards produced at the start of the First World War; others in the series include Russia, Siberia, France, Italy and Belgium and the set would be worth about £12/$22.

*Great Britain*

theme now fetch around £3-£5/$5-$9. Naturally, almost all of the subjects covered in previous chapters have appeared on comic postcards in their time: from the coming of the motor car to the early intrepid aviator; from the scantily-clad girl in her boudoir to what Kipling termed, 'the flannelled fools at the wicket and the muddied oafs in the goals'.

Finally, it should be mentioned that the postcard collector of today need not look exclusively to the publishers of eighty years ago for inspiration. Just by looking in some of the many high street card shops, gift shops, indoor markets and museums and art galleries a wide variety of very fine modern cards can be found. Just as in Edwardian times, the cards of today tend to reflect the society that produces them, therefore preserving that society in pictures for future generations. Currently popular topics, as well as modern versions of old favourites, are depicted by today's photographers and artists, enabling fresh collections to be built up at very modest cost (usually 30-40 pence/50-70 cents per card). Glamour, advertising, royalty, transport, political, rock and pop music, animals and comic cards are just some of the subjects readily available from the ever-increasing number of outlets selling these moderns. All you need to do is just go out and look — it really could not be simpler!

*Below* 'Large-letter' cards bearing names or letters of the alphabet were popular with the Edwardian public. This set also has theatrical interest, as the letters contain the faces of leading actresses of the day.

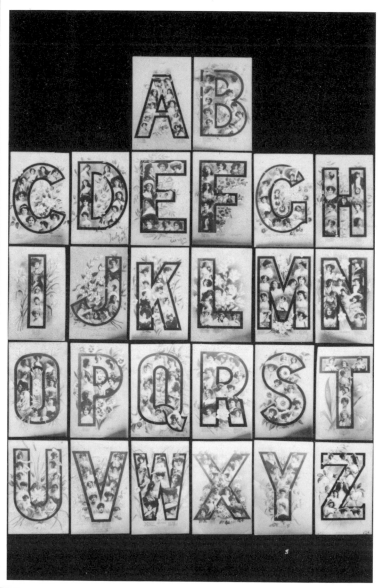

*Below* Bears, both real and as drawn by artists, are a very popular subject with today's collectors. The top example belongs equally in the social history section, the bottom one is from a set of six cards by A. E. Kennedy illustrating the *Goldilocks* story.

*Overleaf* The postcard publishers of today issue a fine range of cards for the collector, some along the same themes as their Edwardian predecessors, others depicting up-to-date subjects or making use of relatively recent techniques such as the airbrush.

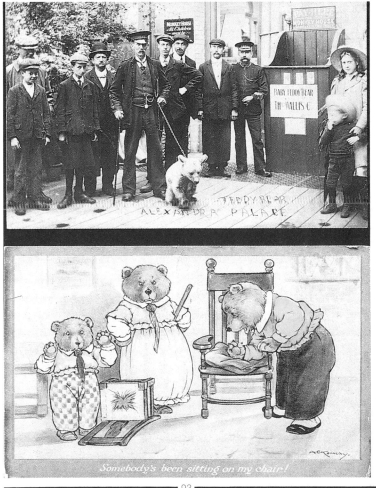

NAGEL
·THE BOOK·

THE ROCKY
HORROR
PICTURE SHOW

**a different
set of jaws**

R RESTRICTED